This book be

(....)

BUG BEEPERS FOR PROMISE KEEPERS

CONNECTING OUR KIDS TO THE VALUES WE HONOR

By Paula Bussard • Illustrated by Dan Maurice

Dear Jesus,
I want to live like a Promise Kid by following your directions.
But sometimes I don't know what to do. Teach me how to follow you.
Help me _____ (name something for which you need
God's help). In your name,
Amen.

Bug Beepers for Promise Keepers
Connecting Our Kids to the Values We Honor

Created by: Paula Bussard
Cover and Text Illustrations by: Dan Maurice
Cover and Text Design: De Leon Design
Editors: Debbie Bible, Marian Oliver

© 1999 Mainstay Church Resources
Published by Mainstay Church Resources
Printed in the United States of America

Mainstay Church Resources' passion is to facilitate revival among God's people by helping pastors help them develop healthy spiritual habits in nine vital areas that always characterize genuine times of spiritual awakening. To support this goal, Mainstay Church Resources uses a C.H.U.R.C.H. strategy to provides practical tools and resources, including the annual 50-Day Spiritual Adventure, the Seasonal Advent Celebration, the 4-Week Festival of Worship, and the Pastor's Toolbox.

CRITTER COUNTY® is a registered trademark of Loveland Communications, Inc. Used by permission. Critter County was codeveloped by Paula Bussard and Christine Wyrtzen through their ministry called Loveland Communications. Their books and tapes have been enjoyed by more than a million children across North America. For additional product or concert information, contact:
Loveland Communications, Inc.
PO Box 7
Loveland, OH 45140
(513) 575-4673
E-mail address: Loveland@Goodnews.net

Unless otherwise noted, Scripture quotations are taken from the International Children's Bible, New Century Version, copyright © 1983, 1986, 1988 by Word Publishing, Dallas, Texas 75039. Used by permission,

Scriptures marked KJV are from the King James Version.

ISBN 1-57849-109-6

"Accelerated spiritual growth for individuals and families"

Helping Pastors
Help People Grow

You have made a wise and eternally significant decision by involving your family in this 50-Day Spiritual Adventure. You are communicating to your child that regular, focused spiritual study is important to you and to your family's growth.

Throughout this Adventure, your child will learn biblical truths and Scripture verses. To make the Adventure more memorable, Sydney, Lester, and many of your child's friends in Critter County will go along. There are eight topics to be studied. The first seven topics are based on the seven promises for adults from the Promise Keepers movement.

These are the things that young Promise Kids are encouraged to do:

1. **Stop and think about Jesus**
2. **Find friends who help them follow Jesus**
3. **Do what Jesus would do**
4. **Make family time important**
5. **Get involved at church**
6. **Accept others as Jesus does**
7. **Help people in the world**
8. **Stay on the Promise Path**

Each week your child will have a memory verse. To help your child learn and retain the scripture, you may use the *Bug Beepers for Promise Keepers* audiotape, which has all eight verses set to music. You may order this tape from Mainstay Church Resources (see page 64). A complete listing of the Adventure memory verses is found on pages 32–33. They are taken from the International Children's Bible.

There is an activity for each of the 50 days of the Adventure, plus two warm-up days. Each page suggests something fun for your child to do to help teach and reinforce the topic for the week. The activity sections are written at a first/second grade reading level. Therefore, preschoolers will need help with directions.

In addition, each page has "Let's Talk About It" discussion questions. These questions are given to open up conversations and teaching opportunities for you. The "Let's Pray About It" section provides guidance to show your child various ways to express himself or herself in conversation with God. And you and your child will enjoy reading more about Critter County in the two stories provided on pages 9–14.

It is the prayer of all who have had a part in developing this activity book for your family that God will use it in a mighty way in the life and spiritual growth of your child. May it be a source of inspiration, training, and fun! Your investment of time and energy will have eternal rewards!

His child and your encourager,

Paula Bussard

Paula Bussard
Loveland Communications, Inc.
PO Box 7
Loveland, OH 45140

· ·

Special note to parents: Rewards for a job well done are important to children as well as adults. Think about something in the way of an incentive to help keep your child motivated to do as much as possible in this activity book.

Oh, one more thing. At the bottom of each page there is a joke or funny fact about animals. You can mail us your favorite joke or fact, too. See page 63.

Sydney the squirrel is a lively, lovable little fellow. He has great big eyes and a heart to match. He is a leader in Critter County.

Sydney loves funny stories. Do you have any jokes to send him?

He also loves to sing and tell others about Jesus.

And he is always willing to help others.

You'll love to hear Sydney sing on the Bug Beepers tape.

His great voice will make it fun to learn about life and God's Word.

Do you love fun? Then you and the lovable lions will be fast friends.
  Lester, the dad, has a big heart and gentle hug. He also has
a hungry stomach. Sometimes he gets scared. And he likes to sing.
In fact, he has written songs that he plays on his guitar.
  His wife, Liona Lou, always makes people feel better. She loves
snappy clothes. She loves to fix her favorite, lion chow, for dinner.
  Their son, Lunchbox, loves baseball, hamburgers, and video games.
Lunchbox reminds us that it can be a lot of fun to be a kid.
But some days can be hard, too. The lessons Lunchbox learns
can help us all to grow.

A tender hug and warm cheese pie are always found
in Grandmother Mouse's kitchen.
She loves to sit and rock the Critter County babies.
  Come to Grandmother Mouse's house for a hug and a story.
She's got just what you need.

Buttons and Boomer are the bug beepers. They like to cheer for people. Follow Buttons and Boomer through the activity book. When you see them, you'll know someone is being a Promise Kid!

On the Bug Beepers tape, they make happy sounds when things go well. And they have an alarm when something could go wrong.

Waves of Joy

"Hey, Dad," yelled Lunchbox. "This is the best vacation we've ever had. I can't believe we get to go whitewater rafting!"

Lester, Liona Lou and Lunchbox all piled into the raft. Lester put the lion chow sandwiches near his seat. Liona Lou put her purse and makeup kit near the back. Lunchbox and his mother tightened their life jackets.

"Here's YOUR life jacket, Lester," said Liona Lou.

"Do we have one for my guitar?" asked Lester with a smile.

Liona Lou and Lunchbox both laughed.

Soon the raft was winding and turning around sharp bends. Big rocks stuck out of the water. Lester had to bend and twist to keep from hitting them. "Wow, this is SO MUCH FUN!" shouted Lunchbox. Just then the raft went around a bend and started down a steep drop.

Suddenly, the front of the raft hit a rock. The raft jerked to the right and got stuck in an old, dead tree.

"Not to worry," said Lester with a smile. "I'll get us out."

As he struggled and tugged, his foot slipped. He fell into the water, knocking his guitar in as well.

"Oh, help, HELP!" screamed Liona Lou.

"I'm fine," assured Lester. "I've got my life jacket on. But my guitar doesn't have one!"

Lester's head bobbed in and out of the water as he made his
way over to the floating guitar.

Liona Lou grabbed her makeup kit. She handed the strap
to Lester so he could hold on. Lunchbox took a paddle and moved
carefully to the end of the raft. "Here, Dad. Hold on to this."

Liona and Lunchbox slowly pulled Lester and the guitar back
to the raft. Lester handed the guitar to Lunchbox. Then he put his leg
over the side. Liona Lou and Lunchbox pulled him into the raft.

"Whew," said Lester, "That was a close one. I almost lost my guitar."

"Were you scared, Daddy?" asked Lunchbox.

"Oh, a little bit. But I knew my life jacket would keep me up.
It was my guitar I was most worried about. And without
you and your mom, I would never have been able to save it.
My, I'm glad I have you both as my family! I love you."

"And we sure love you," said Lunchbox, "and your guitar."
Then they all hugged.

Three Cheers For You

"Ring the bell! She's lost in the woods. Grandmother Mouse is lost in the woods," shouted Sydney.

All the critters came running. Lester brought his flashlight.

"Lunchbox, you search down by the creek. Take Okey Dokey donkey with you. He's new here and doesn't know his way around," said Sydney.

"But I don't want to take him with me," thought Lunchbox. "He's so slow." But Lunchbox didn't want to make more trouble. So he found Okey, and they headed off on the search.

After three hours of looking for Grandmother, the critters were tired. And they had not found her. Sydney was worried. "If we don't find her soon, the heat will make her sick," he said.

Liona Lou had brought sandwiches. The critters ate as fast as they could. "Let's keep looking," said Lester.

The critters each went a different way. Lunchbox thought, "I'll never find her. This big, dumb donkey is slowing me down. And his long ears keep blocking my view."

Soon the sun started to go down behind the mountains. Still, there was no sign of the dear grandmother. Everyone was getting very worried. Suddenly, Okey Dokey said, "Stop, Lunchbox. Listen!" Lunchbox stood still.

"I thought I heard a groan from over there," said Okey. He pointed to a big rock.

"I didn't hear anything," Lunchbox said. "But let's check it out."

The two critters walked closer to the rock. They both heard Grandmother Mouse's calls for help.

"There she is," said Okey. "I'll stay here with her and you go for help." Lunchbox took off as fast as he could. He brought everyone back to the rock.

"How did you find her?" Sydney asked Lunchbox.

"I didn't," said Lunchbox. "Okey heard her crying for help. His big ears made it easy for him to hear her. I guess God made each of us different for a reason. And I think I need to learn to accept those who are not like me."

"I think you have guessed right," answered Sydney. "But now, let's take care of Grandmother Mouse."

The critters made her a soft bed on Okey Dokey's back. That way she could have a comfortable ride home. She felt much better the next morning. Dr. Duck had given her some medicine. And she had eaten some cheese soup. There's nothing quite like cheese soup to make a mouse feel better.

Welcome to the 50-Day Adventure in Critter County. Sydney the squirrel, Lester, Liona Lou, and Lunchbox are glad you are here. Do you see Buttons and Boomer the bug beepers? They will be helping you during the Adventure. You will be learning many new things about Jesus. During the first week, you will learn how to stop and think about Jesus.

Now, draw yourself somewhere in this picture.

Be sure to come back tomorrow!

Oh, one more thing. On each page there is a joke or funny fact about animals. You can mail us your favorite joke or fact, too. See page 63.

A mole can dig a tunnel as long as a football field in one night.

Buttons and Boomer love to see children showing how they love Jesus. In this picture, they see someone who stopped to think about Jesus. Connect the dots to see what this person is doing.

After you connect the dots, color the picture. You might want to use lots of orange and yellow for the bug beepers.

**Why did the skeleton cross the road?
To get to the body shop.**

Day 1 • Sunday

It's Sunday in Critter County. We want to begin this Adventure by learning the Memory Verse for Week 1. It is printed below. One meaning of the verse is "Stop and think about Jesus." You will learn some ways to do this. Yesterday, you learned that one way to do this is to work in your activity book. What is another way you can think about Jesus?

Draw or write your answer on the blackboard.

Say the memory verse out loud. Every time you say it, draw a happy face by the verse.

Let's Talk About It:
• Tell some other ways you can stop and think about Jesus.
• By stopping and thinking about Jesus we show him we _____ him.

Let's Pray About It:
Pray the Promise Kids Prayer on page 2. Ask Jesus to help you remember to stop and think about him each day.

Memory Verse:
God says, "Be quiet and know that I am God." Psalm 46:10

How do you get down from an elephant?
You don't. You get down from a duck.

Day 2 • Monday

Friends like to be together. It is the same with Jesus. We can get to know him better by spending time with him. What are some ways we can do this?

Look at the pictures. Circle the children who are stopping and thinking about Jesus. Underline the one doing what you will do this week.

Let's Talk About It:
• Read Matthew 19:14 with your child.
• Why is it a good idea to stop and think about Jesus each day?

Let's Pray About It:
When you pray today, thank Jesus for being your friend.

Memory Verse:
God says, "Be quiet and know that I am God." Psalm 46:10

What is black and white and red all over?
A sunburned zebra.

Day 3 • Tuesday

Lunchbox has something for us to remember when we think about Jesus today. Read his sign. What is your favorite thing that Jesus made? **Draw or write about it in the empty picture frame.**

Tomorrow, Lunchbox will give us another idea to use as we think about Jesus.

Let's Talk About It:
• Read John 1:3 with your child.
• What are some other things that Jesus has made?

Let's Pray About It:
As you pray today, remember to thank Jesus for some of the things that he has made.

Memory Verse:
God says, "Be quiet and know that I am God." Psalm 46:10

What vegetable do you get when King Kong walks through your garden? Squash.

Day 4 • Wednesday

When you think about Jesus today, Lunchbox wants you to remember that "Jesus loves me." This is amazing when you think how many people are in the world. But Jesus loves each one, including you.

Look at the map below and ask someone to help you find where you live. Then fill in the blanks.

My name is _____ and Jesus loves me.

I live in _____ and Jesus knows where that is.

I am _____ years old. Jesus has known and loved me since before I was born.

Let's Talk About It:
• Read and discuss John 3:16 with your child.
• What has Jesus done to show his love for you?

Let's Pray About It:
As you pray the Promise Kids Prayer (page 2), ask Jesus to help you remember how much he loves you.

Memory Verse:
God says, "Be quiet and know that I am God." Psalm 46:10

What do you call a 5,000 pound gorilla?
Sir.

Day 5 • Thursday

What truth is Lunchbox reminding us of today? That's right. Jesus listens to EVERY prayer. He may not answer them all with a "yes." But he hears and answers each one. When you listen to someone, what body part do you use?

Look at the ears below. Draw a line from the ears to the head where they belong.

When you stop and think about Jesus, you can use your ears and mind. To use your mind means to be still and quiet. You can do something like look at Bible stories or listen to Bible songs.

Let's Talk About It:
• Read Psalm 34:15 with your child.
• Does Jesus always hear us when we pray to him?
• Does he always answer our prayers "yes"? Why or why not?

Let's Pray About It:
As you pray today, thank Jesus for always hearing your prayers. Ask him to help you trust him when he answers your prayers with a "no" or a "wait."

Memory Verse:
God says, "Be quiet and know that I am God." Psalm 46:10

A hippopotamus is born under water and can run faster than a man.

21

Day 6 • Friday

The Bible tells us that Jesus takes care of us like a _____ .

To find out what goes in the blank, connect the dots.

Now, write your name on one of the sheep. Think about Jesus today as your Good Shepherd.

Let's Talk About It:
• Spend a little time in John 10:14–15 and talk with your child about the role of a shepherd.
• How does it make you feel to know that Jesus is your Shepherd?

Let's Pray About It:
Pray the Promise Kids Prayer. Ask Jesus to help you remember that he is your Good Shepherd. And don't forget to thank him.

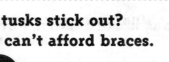

Memory Verse:
God says, "Be quiet and know that I am God." Psalm 46:10

Why do elephant tusks stick out?
Because their parents can't afford braces.

Days 7 and 8 • Saturday and Sunday

It is the beginning of Week 2 of the Adventure. Your Critter County friends want to help you learn a new Memory Verse. They have divided it into four parts. **Copy each part from the verse at the bottom of the page. Or, for preschoolers, say each part. As you learn each part, color one of the animals.**

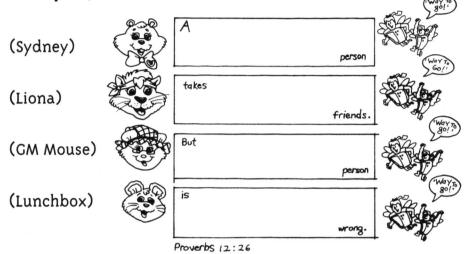

(Sydney)   A _____ person

(Liona)   takes _____ friends.

(GM Mouse)   But _____ person

(Lunchbox)   is _____ wrong.

Proverbs 12:26

Your Critter County friends are good friends to have. Why? Because they help you follow Jesus. Following Jesus means doing what Jesus would do. Friends who help you follow Jesus often give good advice. During the week, we will learn about other friends who help us follow Jesus.

Let's Talk About It:
• What is advice?
• What kind of friends give good advice?

Let's Pray About It:
Use the Promise Kids Prayer. Ask Jesus to help you find friends who can give you good advice.

Memory Verse:
A good person takes advice from his friends. But an evil person is easily led to do wrong. Proverbs 12:26

What is smarter than a talking parrot?
A spelling bee.

Day 9 • Monday

Today, we are going to learn how friends can help us by giving good advice.

Grandmother Mouse is watching Lunchbox while his parents have gone shopping. But Lunchbox has a problem. One of his friends called him a mean name. What should he do? Grandmother is giving him some advice. **Circle the two pieces of advice that are the best. Then you can be a good friend to Lunchbox, too!**

Call your friend a mean name, too.

Tell your friend that you do not like to be called mean names.

I know that your feelings are hurt. But ask Jesus to help you forgive your friend.

Let's Talk About It:
• Who gives you advice?
• How do you know if the advice is good?

Let's Pray About It:
Pray the Promise Kids Prayer today. Ask Jesus to show you how to tell good advice from bad advice.

Memory Verse:
A good person takes advice from his friends. But an evil person is easily led to do wrong. Proverbs 12:26

Jake the Snake: "Boy, I hope I'm not poisonous!"
Blake the Snake: "Why is that?" Jake the Snake: "Because I just bit my tongue."

Day 10 • Tuesday

Yesterday we learned about good advice. Listening to good advice can help us follow Jesus. Today, we are going to learn about special friends who help us follow Jesus. Who are these special friends? Parents and teachers.

Look at the two pictures. Finish each one. Do you see how the parent and teacher are helping someone follow Jesus? Below each picture, write (or tell) what the parent or teacher is doing. Then color each picture.

_____   _____

_____   _____

Let's Talk About It:
• What other ways do parents and teachers help us follow Jesus?
• Name some other friends who help you follow Jesus.

Let's Pray About It:
In your prayer time, remember to thank Jesus for parents and teachers.

Memory Verse:
A good person takes advice from his friends. But an evil person is easily led to do wrong. Proverbs 12:26

Why do hummingbirds hum?
Because they don't know the words.

Day 11 • Wednesday

Besides parents and teachers, who are some other friends who can help you follow Jesus?

Fill in the vowels. The vowels are: A E I O U.
(Preschoolers may need help on this page.)

  __ L D __ R   __ D __ L T S

P __ S T __ R S

S C H __ __ L   M __ T __ S

C H __ R C H   F R __ __ N D S

Let's Talk About It:
• Name some school or church friends who give you good advice.
• Do you help your friends follow Jesus? How?

Let's Pray About It:
As you pray today, thank Jesus for the friends who help you follow him.

Memory Verse:
A good person takes advice from his friends.
But an evil person is easily led to do wrong. Proverbs 12:26

What did the baby chick say to his mom at bedtime?
"I'm egg-zhausted!"

Day 12 • Thursday

Sydney and Lunchbox are good friends. They often give each other good advice. Do you have a friend who gives you good advice?

Draw a picture of you and your friend with Sydney and Lunchbox.

Let's Talk About It:
• How does your friend help you follow Jesus?
• How can you help your friend follow Jesus?

Let's Pray About It:
Pray for the special friend whose picture you drew today.

Memory Verse:
A good person takes advice from his friends. But an evil person is easily led to do wrong. Proverbs 12:26

What do you call flowers that are really good friends?
Best buds.

Day 13 • Friday

Sydney is glad that you have learned about friends who help you follow Jesus. But he wants to know if you can tell good friends from bad friends. **Look at the pictures below. Which friends are good friends? Draw a smiley face beside them.**

Let's Talk About It:
• Good friends help you do what is _____.
• How can you be a good friend?

Let's Pray About It:
Pray the Promise Kids Prayer. Ask Jesus to help you choose good friends.

Memory Verse:
A good person takes advice from his friends. But an evil person is easily led to do wrong. Proverbs 12:26

What does a duck do when he flies upside down?
He quacks up.

Days 14 and 15 • Saturday and Sunday

It's time to learn a new Memory Verse. This week we will study Hebrews 12:1. Read the verse at the bottom of the page. The word "remove" means "to get rid of." The word "sin" means "the wrong things we do."

Today, you can help Lunchbox get rid of some wrong things. Use your pencil or crayon to help him walk to the ice cream shop.
When you come to a sin or wrong thing, put a big X on it. Every time you put an X on something, say the Memory Verse out loud. Getting rid of sins is one way we can do what Jesus wants us to do.

Let's Talk About It:
• What does the word "remove" mean?
• What is sin?

Let's Pray About It:
Pray the Promise Kids Prayer. Ask Jesus to help you get rid of a sin (wrong thing) in your life. Some examples of sins are: lying, stealing, cheating, hurting other people on purpose with words or actions, and so on.

Memory Verse:
We should remove the sin that so easily catches us. Hebrews 12:1

Why did the hen lay an egg?
Because if she dropped it, it would break.

Day 16 • Monday

Yesterday, we learned that getting rid of sins is something that Jesus wants us to do. But how do we do this? Liona Lou is standing by a mirror with the answer.

Hold this page up to your mirror to read the answer.

1 By asking Jesus to forgive us.
2 By making decisions to stop doing wrong.
3 By asking Jesus to help us do what is right.

Let's Talk About It:
• How do we get rid of sin?
• Is there a sin you need to talk about?

Let's Pray About It:
Pray today and thank Jesus for his willingness to help you get rid of your sins.

Memory Verse:
We should remove the sin that so easily catches us. Hebrews 12:1

Have you sent your favorite joke to Sydney? (See page 63.) Please do it today. Sydney and the critters love to laugh!

Day 17 • Tuesday

We have been talking about getting rid of sins this week. Yesterday, we learned that we need to go to Jesus with our sins. Today, we want to learn about a word that goes with sin. The word is "temptation" [temp-TAY-shun]. Do you know what the word means? Lester is holding a sign to help you.

Use the code to figure out what the sign says. (Preschoolers may need help on this page.)

Temptation is:

B __ __ N G __ N C __ __ R __ G __ D
  2   3   2   4 5   1   2

T __ D __ W H __ T __ S W R __ N G.
  4   4   1   3   4

Code: 1=A; 2=E; 3=I; 4=O; 5=U.

Everyone is tempted. Being tempted is not sin. But what can you do when you are tempted? Ask Jesus to help you stand strong and do what is right.

Let's Talk About It:
• Is it wrong to be tempted?
• What can you do when you are tempted?

Let's Pray About It:
Pray the Promise Kids Prayer. Ask Jesus to help you to do what is right. What's right is what he would do.

Memory Verse:
We should remove the sin that so easily catches us. Hebrews 12:1

**Why can't a cat use the computer?
It keeps chasing the mouse.**

WEEK 1

God says, "Be quiet and
know that I am God."
Psalm 46:10

WEEK 2

A good person takes advice from
his friends. But an evil person
is easily led to do wrong.
Proverbs 12:26

WEEK 3

We should remove the sin
that so easily catches us.
Hebrews 12:1

WEEK 4

"Honor your father and mother."
Ephesians 6:2–3

WEEK 5

You should meet together
and encourage each other.
Hebrews 10:25

WEEK 6

People look at the outside of a person,
but the Lord looks at the heart.
1 Samuel 16:7

WEEK 7

You should be a light for other people.
Matthew 5:16

WEEK 8

You (God) will teach me God's way to live.
Psalm 16:11

Day 18 • Wednesday

We've been talking about sin and how to get rid of it. Why? Because that is what Jesus wants us to do. And because we love him, we want to please him.

Grandmother Mouse has stopped in today. She will help us learn other ways to be strong Christians. These things will help us stand strong when we are tempted.

Connect Grandmother Mouse's sewing stitches to read her message. (Preschoolers may need help with reading the message.)

Did you find Grandmother Mouse's message?
Now, remember to do it!

Let's Talk About It:
• Why is it good to read your Bible and pray?
• How can that make you a strong Christian?

Let's Pray About It:
Pray the Promise Kids Prayer. Ask Jesus to help you learn from your Bible and to pray often.

Memory Verse:
We should remove the sin that so easily catches us. Hebrews 12:1

**What do rain clouds wear under their silver linings?
Thunderwear.**

Day 19 • Thursday

Jesus wants us to choose to do what is right. Sometimes this is hard. But we can do it with Jesus' help.

Look at the boy on this page. Someone has hurt his feelings. What would be a right thing he could do? Each door has a list of choices. Draw a circle around the door with the best choices. Then color that door. On door #3 write or draw your own idea of what the boy could do.

Let's Talk About It:
• What do you do when someone hurts your feelings?
• What would Jesus do if someone hurt his feelings?

Let's Pray About It:
Ask Jesus to help you do what he would do when someone hurts your feelings.

Memory Verse:
We should remove the sin that so easily catches us. Hebrews 12:1

Where do books sleep?
Under their covers.

Day 20 • Friday

This week we have learned many things. What is the most important thing? We are learning how to be like . . .

Connect the dots.

Let's Talk About It:
• What book tells us about Jesus?
• How can we be more like Jesus?

Let's Pray About It:
Pray and ask Jesus to help you be more like him.

Memory Verse:
We should remove the sin that so easily catches us. Hebrews 12:1

Why is a pencil like a riddle?
It's no good without a point.

Days 21 and 22 • Saturday and Sunday

It's Memory Verse time again. This week's verse is easy to learn but can be hard to do. How do we honor our parents? By obeying and loving them. Say the verse out loud several times until you know it. Then, look for ways to show your parents that you honor them.

Lunchbox has found a way to honor his mom. He has drawn a picture of her. He has written a note. You can do this, too.
Draw a picture of your mom. You may want to print the memory verse under the picture you draw.

Let's Talk About It:
• Why can it be hard to honor our parents?
• Who can help us?

Let's Pray About It:
Pray the Promise Kids Prayer. Ask Jesus to help you honor your parents.

Memory Verse:
"Honor your father and mother." Ephesians 6:2

**What does the ocean say when it sees the shore?
Nothing, it just waves.**

Day 23 • Monday

Do you know what we do in Critter County to celebrate our families? We have a "Glad-I-Gotcha-Day." Would you like to have a "Glad-I-Gotcha-Day" at your house? Here are some ideas:

1. Make a poster for the kitchen. Write "I'm So Glad I Gotcha." Then put everyone's name in your family on it. Don't forget your pets. You might need help drawing pictures or writing.

2. Help with jobs around the house. When you are finished, hug the person you helped. Then say with a smile, "I'm Glad-I-Gotcha."

3. Come up with your own ideas. List or draw them on the blank paper.

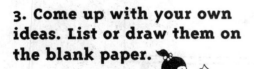

Let's Talk About It:
• Do you like to get hugs and be told that you are special?
• How does it make you feel?

Let's Pray About It:
As you pray, ask Jesus to show you ways you can love your family.

Memory Verse:
"Honor your father and mother." Ephesians 6:2

How do you catch a squirrel?
Climb up a tree and act like a nut.

Day 24 • Tuesday

Families come in all shapes and sizes. Look at the families in the picture. Some have skin. Others have fur. Some have one parent and others have two. Some have a grandparent living with them.

They all look like they enjoy being together. **Count how many children are in the pictures. How many parents and grandparents are there? Write the numbers on the lines. Then color the pictures.**

Children

_____

Parents and Grandparents

_____

Let's Talk About It:
• What is a family?
• What would it feel like not to have a family?

Let's Pray About It:
Pray today and thank Jesus for your family.

Memory Verse:
"Honor your father and mother." Ephesians 6:2

What's the difference between a bus driver and a cold?
One knows the stops and the other stops the nose.

Day 25 • Wednesday

Grandparents love to read stories to their grandchildren. Look at Grandmother Mouse. She is reading a Bible story to her granddaughter.

What is your favorite Bible story? Draw a picture of it in Grandmother Mouse's book. Then color the picture.

Let's Talk About It:
• Do you like it when your grandparents (relatives) read to you?
• What else can you learn from your grandparents (relatives)?

Let's Pray About It:
When you pray, be sure to thank Jesus for your relatives.

Memory Verse:
"Honor your father and mother." Ephesians 6:2

**What has four wheels and flies?
A garbage truck.**

Day 26 • Thursday

Families are like a team. They play together and work hard together. And if everyone does his or her part, the family can be happy. The Lions are a happy family because each person helps to do the work.

Look at the picture. Liona Lou had a big party. There is a mess in her living room. It would take one person a long time to clean up. But look! Lester and Lunchbox are coming to help. Show them where to put everything. Draw a line to the place each item belongs.

Let's Talk About It:
• How do you feel when you have to do too much work by yourself?
• Why should families work and help each other?

Let's Pray About It:
Pray the Promise Kids Prayer. Ask Jesus to help you do your part to make your family a happy one.

Memory Verse:
"Honor your father and mother." Ephesians 6:2

Why is it silly to be afraid of a dogwood tree?
Because it's all bark and no bite.

Day 27 • Friday

Families were made to love and help each other. And Grandmother Mouse is sure glad that she has a family. She fell and broke her hip. She has to stay in bed for six weeks. Then she will have to use mouse crutches and a walker. Poor Grandmother Mouse.

Her Critter County family is bringing her dinner, and Lester is fixing her door. How do you think their helping makes her feel? Now, there is something YOU can do to help her feel better! Send your favorite joke to her. She will giggle till her tail just about wiggles off the bed.

Write to:
Grandmother Mouse
Critter County
PO Box 30
Wheaton, IL 60189

Let's Talk About It:
• Have you ever been sick? Who took care of you?
• How could you help when someone in your family gets sick?

Let's Pray About It:
As you pray, ask Jesus to help someone in your family who is sick or in trouble.

Memory Verse:
"Honor your father and mother." Ephesians 6:2

What do you get when you pass a duck and a cow?
Quackers and milk.

Days 28 and 29 • Saturday and Sunday

Another weekend is here. That means it's time to learn another Memory Verse. **The verse is printed at the bottom of the page. What do you think it means? (Hold this page up to your mirror to find out.)**

It means that we should meet together at church with church friends.

Now, here is a way to learn the verse:

1. First, say the verse out loud. Then count the windows in the church. Write the number on the line.
2. Say the verse again. Then count the trees. Write the number on the line.
3. After you say the verse again, count the animals. Write that number.

windows _____

trees _____

animals _____

Let's Talk About It:
• Why do you like to go to church?
• What is your favorite part of church time?

Let's Pray About It:
As you pray, remember to thank Jesus for your church.

Memory Verse:
You should meet together and encourage each other. Hebrews 10:25

How did the farmer count his cows?
With a "cowculator."

Day 30 • Monday

At church you get to be with family and friends.
Look at everyone enjoying church at the Critter County Chapel.
Do you see Pastor Penguin? He is leading a song. And everyone is joining in.

Look for all of the things that start with the letter "s." Put a circle around each one.

Let's Talk About It:
• How does going to church help you grow as a Christian?
• How would you feel if you had no church? Why?

Let's Pray About It:
Pray the Promise Kids Prayer. Ask Jesus to help you grow as a Christian.

Memory Verse:
You should meet together and encourage each other. Hebrews 10:25

Who do birds marry?
Their tweet hearts.

Day 31 • Tuesday

Do you like to draw and color? Do you enjoy singing, or are you taking music lessons? Did you know that you can use your talents at church?

If you like to draw, ask your teacher if you can help draw pictures for a lesson. If you sing, join the children's choir.

Look at the children in the picture. They are using their talents at church. Color the picture using the code.

1—red

2—green

3—blue

4—orange

5—yellow

6—purple

Let's Talk About It:
• What talents do you have?
• How could you use your talents at church?

Let's Pray About It:
Pray the Promise Kids Prayer. Ask Jesus to help you use your talents at church.

Memory Verse:
You should meet together and encourage each other. Hebrews 10:25

What did the barber say to the sad rabbit?
Are you having a bad hare day?

Day 32 • Wednesday

Writing letters and making cards for people can be a lot of fun.
And it encourages people, too.

Have you ever made a card for a church teacher or friend?
Look at the beautiful card that Sydney made. It is for Pastor Penguin.

Dear Pastor, Thank You for being my pastor.

You can make a card, too. To do this, use a plain piece of paper.
Write or draw on it. Then give it to someone
who works at your church.

Let's Talk About It:
• What is this week's Memory Verse? Can you say it all by yourself?
• What else could you do to encourage someone in your church?

Let's Pray About It:
Pray the Promise Kids Prayer. Ask Jesus to help you think of ways
to encourage people in your church.

Memory Verse:
You should meet together and encourage each other. Hebrews 10:25

What did one elevator say to the other elevator?
I think I'm coming down with something.

Day 33 • Thursday

Did you know that your church is like a team? It's true. When everybody does their job, then the church wins.

Look at the Critter County Chapel team. It looks like everyone is having a good time, doesn't it? Pastor Penguin is like the coach. He helps everyone do their jobs. And, as you can see, this church team needs YOU. **Connect the dots.**

Let's Talk About It:
• What kinds of things does your family do to help your church?
• What can you do?

Let's Pray About It:
Pray the Promise Kids Prayer. Ask Jesus to help you discover ways to help at church.

Memory Verse:
You should meet together and encourage each other. Hebrews 10:25

What do turkeys have that no other bird has?
Baby turkeys.

Day 34 • Friday

One way to show our love for God is to give money to our church. Let's make a bank to help us save some money for church.

Look at the bank Buttons and Boomer helped Lunchbox make. You can make one just like it.

After you are finished, start putting money inside the bank each week.

Let's Talk About It:
• Why does God want us to give money to our church?
• What does your church do with the money that people give?

Let's Pray About It:
Ask Jesus to help you have a happy heart when you give money to your church.

Memory Verse:
You should meet together and encourage each other. Hebrews 10:25

Sheep will not drink from running water. That's why the twenty-third psalm says, "He leadeth me beside the still waters." (KJV)

Days 35 and 36 • Saturday and Sunday

Today is Memory Verse day. Read the verse at the bottom of the page. What do you think it means?

Draw a line to match each part of the verse with its meaning.

People look at
the outside of a person

God cares about
what a person
thinks and feels.

but the Lord
looks at the heart

People care about
how much a person has or
what color his or her skin is.

Now, draw a circle around the child who is practicing the verse.

Let's Talk About It:
• Do you know people who are different from you?
• How are they different?

Let's Pray About It:
When you pray, ask Jesus to help you remember that everybody is important to him.

Memory Verse:
People look at the outside of a person, but the Lord looks
at the heart. 1 Samuel 16:7

What do cows do on a Saturday night?
They go to the MOOOOOVIES!

Day 37 • Monday

Yesterday, we learned something about people. They have an inside and an outside. They are kind of like the box Sydney is holding. It's easy to see what is on the outside. But you can't always know what is on the inside. And it is the inside of people that is most important!

Sydney wants you to guess what is in his box.

Here are two hints:
1. It is long and flat and has a wrapper.
2. It starts out hard, but gets soft.

Send your guesses to Sydney. His address is on the mailbox. If you get the right answer, he will send you a surprise. Be sure to print your name and address neatly. Then Moose the mailman can read it.

Sydney, Critter County, P.O. Box 30 Wheaton, IL 60189

Let's Talk About It:
• Which part of a person did God say was most important? The inside or the outside?
• Do you have friends who are different on the outside from you? How are they different?

Let's Pray About It:
Pray the Promise Kids Prayer. Ask Jesus to help you value the inside of a person more than the outside.

Memory Verse:
People look at the outside of a person, but the Lord looks at the heart. 1 Samuel 16:7

**Male moose have antlers seven feet across.
The antlers often weigh sixty pounds.**

Day 38 • Tuesday

It's party time in Critter County. And it looks like everyone is having a great time.

Look at the different ways the critters are dressed. Look at the different kinds of foods. Lunchbox likes his lion chow. The squirrels love their nuts. Liona Lou has popcorn. And Lester loves his critter fritters.

Imagine how boring it would be if everybody were the same. I'm glad God made people different, aren't you?

Color the picture.

Let's Talk About It:
• What would the world be like if everyone looked EXACTLY the same?
• Why do you think God makes each person different?

Let's Pray About It:
As you pray, ask Jesus to help you love people the way he does.

Memory Verse:
People look at the outside of a person, but the Lord looks at the heart. 1 Samuel 16:7

What has ten legs, ten arms, and five heads?
Five people.

Day 39 • Wednesday

Some of the critters in the county need to learn and practice this week's Memory Verse. Do you see how they are treating Okey Dokey donkey? They are making fun of his long, droopy ears. He feels embarrassed and angry. Would you read the Memory Verse for them?

Put an X on the children who are not being kind.
Draw a circle around the ones who are being kind.
Then color the picture.

Let's Talk About It:
• Do you know anyone whom other children make fun of?
• How do you treat this person?

Let's Pray About It:
Pray the Promise Kids Prayer. Ask Jesus to help you treat others kindly, even people who are different.

Memory Verse:
People look at the outside of a person, but the Lord looks at the heart. 1 Samuel 16:7

What goes ha, ha, ha, plop?
Someone laughing his head off!!

Day 40 • Thursday

God made animals different because he likes variety.

Variety means "lots of different kinds." Imagine if God had made only flies. Going to the zoo wouldn't be much fun!

Look at these animals. Draw a line from the animal to the sound that the animal makes.

baaa

Moo

Meow

roar

God also made people different from each other. He wanted our world to be an interesting place. That is why he made so many different kinds of people.

Let's Talk About It:
• Most people talk with their mouths, but some use their hands. Why do they do that?
• How can you show kindness to someone who doesn't speak your language?

Let's Pray About It:
As you pray today, think of someone who talks differently than you do. Ask Jesus to help you show kindness to that person.

Memory Verse:
People look at the outside of a person, but the Lord looks at the heart. 1 Samuel 16:7

Remember to write to Sydney. Tell him what you think is in his box (page 50).

What is a frog's favorite drink?
Croaka-Cola.

Day 41 • Friday

Most people have two legs, two eyes, a nose, and a mouth. But we all look different.

Connect the dots so you can see the lion family.

Notice how each one looks different. But they are one family. And they love each other very much.

Let's Talk About It:
• How do you look different from your family members?
• How do you look the same?

Let's Pray About It:
Pray the Promise Kids Prayer. Ask Jesus to help you value how your family members are different.

Memory Verse:
People look at the outside of a person, but the Lord looks at the heart. 1 Samuel 16:7

What always falls but never gets hurt?
Rain.

Days 42 and 43 • Saturday and Sunday

It's a bright day in Critter County. That's because we are learning a new Memory Verse today. It is at the bottom of the page. Read it to yourself.

Now, look at the lights in Liona Lou's den.
Draw a circle around each light that you see.
There may be some outside of the house, too.
Then color the picture to really brighten up her den.

Let's Talk About It:
• How do lights help us?
• How can a person be like a light?
• What can you do to help others want to know Jesus?

Let's Pray About It:
Pray the Promise Kids Prayer. Ask Jesus to help you be a light to lead others to him.

Memory Verse:
You should be a light for other people. Matthew 5:16

What has no beginning, no end, and nothing in the middle?
A doughnut.

Day 44 • Monday

Grandmother Mouse has a grandson. Many years ago, he decided
that God wanted him to travel and tell people about Jesus.
That is how he could be a light for other people.
So he packed his suitcase and Bible and went to the boat.
As he was getting on the boat, he realized he was missing six things.

**Put a circle around each of these six items so that he can find them:
watch, stuffed cat, map, cheese, toothbrush, and coat.**

Let's Talk About It:
• Why do we send missionaries to faraway places?
• Would you ever like to go on a mission adventure? Where?

Let's Pray About It:
When you pray today, ask Jesus to be with the missionaries
around the world. Ask him to take good care of them so they can
help others.

Memory Verse:
You should be a light for other people. Matthew 5:16

**What is full of holes but can still hold water?
A sponge.**

Day 45 · Tuesday

Some of us can't go to other places and tell people about Jesus. Some of us need to stay at home. But we can help by writing to missionaries.

Ask a parent to help you find out who your church missionaries are. Then write a letter or draw a picture. They will be happy to know that you are thinking about and praying for them.

Let's Talk About It:
• What do you think it is like to be a missionary?
• What else can you do to help the missionaries?

Let's Pray About It:
Pray today for a missionary family that you know about. If you don't know of one, then locate a country on a map and pray for it.

Memory Verse:
You should be a light for other people. Matthew 5:16

**What do you get if you cross a fish with an elephant?
Swimming trunks.**

Day 46 • Wednesday

Sydney has a quiz for you today.
Circle Yes if the sentence is true. Circle No if the sentence is false.

1. Sunday school teachers can be missionaries.

YES   NO

2. Children can be missionaries.

YES   NO

3. To be a missionary you have to travel far away.

YES   NO

4. A missionary is anyone who tells others about Jesus.

YES   NO

5. Telling others about Jesus is one way to be a light to other people.

YES   NO

How did you do? Check your answers here.

Answers: YES, YES, NO, YES, YES

Let's Talk About It:
• Have you ever told anyone about Jesus? Who?
• Besides talking, what are some other ways to be a missionary?

Let's Pray About It:
Pray the Promise Kids Prayer. Ask Jesus to help you find ways to be a light to other people.

Memory Verse:
You should be a light for other people. Matthew 5:16

Male monkeys lose the hair on their heads in the same way men do.

Day 47 • Thursday

Jesus loves all the children in the whole world. And he loves for us to tell others about him. Look at these pictures of people in faraway places. Did you notice that some live in different kinds of houses?

Draw a line from each child to the house that he or she might live in.

Let's Talk About It:
• If we go to a faraway place to tell others about Jesus, we might have to live differently. What are some things that might be different?
• Would it be hard to live in a different place? Why or why not?

Let's Pray About It:
Pray the Promise Kids Prayer. Ask Jesus to help you tell others about him.

Memory Verse:
You should be a light for other people. Matthew 5:16

Why are flowers so lazy?
Because they are usually in beds.

Day 48 • Friday

Today we get to pick apples and learn another Memory Verse. Lester is up on the ladder looking for just the right apples. Grandmother Mouse is going to make a Bible Verse Apple Pie.

Draw a circle around the apples he should pick so that she can make her pie. Then color the picture. (For preschoolers, make an enlarged copy of this page. Then cut out the apples with verse words on them. Have your preschooler lay the apples in order using the verse at the bottom of the page as a guide.)

Let's Talk About It:
• What things can you do to live God's way?
• Who has promised to help you?

Let's Pray About It:
Pray the Promise Kids Prayer. Ask Jesus to help you live his way.

Memory Verse:
You (God) will teach me God's way to live. Psalm 16:11

**What's the only thing worse than finding a worm in your apple?
Finding half a worm.**

Day 49 • Saturday

God wants us to live his way. When we live his way we stay on the Promise Path. How can we do that? With God's help. Remember the Memory Verse from yesterday? This is God's promise to you.

Look at the maze. These children need help living God's way. Use a pencil or crayon to help them.

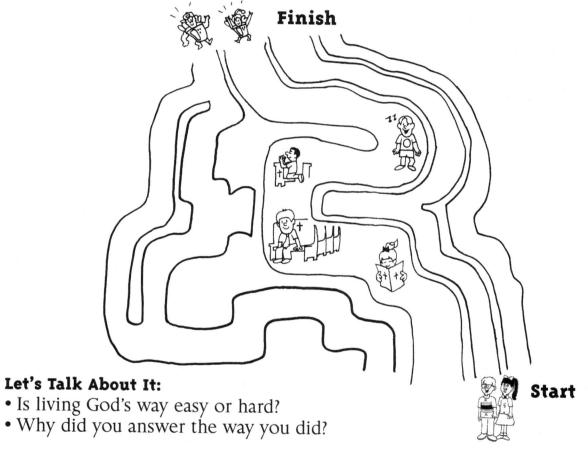

Let's Talk About It:
• Is living God's way easy or hard?
• Why did you answer the way you did?

Let's Pray About It:
When you pray, thank Jesus for helping you to know how to live his way.

Memory Verse:
You (God) will teach me God's way to live. Psalm 16:11

What do you call a cow with no legs?
Ground beef.

Day 50 • Sunday

Jesus died on the cross for our sins. But he rose from the grave! He is still alive. Telling people about him is important. Do you tell your friends about him and how much he loves them?

Sometimes people can write letters to tell others about Jesus. Look at the letter that Sydney wrote to a friend. **Trace over his words. (Preschoolers may need help reading the letter after they have traced the letters.)**

Dear Friend
.. am writing to let you know
He sent Jesus to die on the cross
so your sins could be forgiven.
Would you like to know more?
I would be happy to talk with you.
Love,
Sydney.

You may want to write a real letter to someone. Tell that person about Jesus.

Let's Talk About It:
• What have you enjoyed most on this Adventure?
• What have you learned from Sydney and your other Critter County friends?

Let's Pray About It:
As you pray, thank God for choosing you to be his child.

Memory Verse:
You (God) will teach me God's way to live. Psalm 16:11

See you next year for another fun ADVENTURE.

We need a joke from you. We might even put it in one of our books. Turn to the next page to see how to send your favorites.

Got a Joke a Squirrel Would Love?

Uh oh! Sydney the squirrel is running out of jokes! He loves jokes. Can you help? Send him your favorite joke.

Write your joke in the frame that sydney is holding. Then have your mom or dad fill out the form on the next page. Send it to the Critter County Post Office in care of Mainstay Church Resources. The Critters will send you the very first Critter County tape with Christine Wyrtzen and Sydney the squirrel.

Please Send Us Your Free Critter County Audiotape, *Critter County* Featuring Christine Wyrtzen and Introducing Sydney the Squirrel

Please send us the following additional Critter County products:

Item	Title	Price	Quantity	Total
451R	Bug Beepers for Promise Keepers Critter County Scripture Memory Songs	$7.00	_____	_____
8441	Larry-Boy! and the Fib from Outer Space! VeggieTales Video	$15.00	_____	_____
2840	Critter County Power Buddies Children's Activity Book	$7.00	_____	_____
451K	Critter County Power Buddies Children's Scripture Memory Audiotape	$7.00	_____	_____
2740	Critter County Clubhouse Children's Activity Book	$6.00	_____	_____
450X	Critter County Clubhouse Children's Scripture Memory Audiotape	$6.00	_____	_____
2640	Pack Up My Backpack Children's Activity Book	$6.00	_____	_____
450S	Pack Up My Backpack Children's Scripture Memory Audiotape	$6.00	_____	_____

Subtotal $ ⬭

Add 10% for UPS shipping/handling ($4.00 minimum) .... $ _____

Canadian or Illinois residents add 7% GST/sales tax .... $ _____

Total (subtotal + shipping + tax) $ ⬭

Total Amount Enclosed $ ⬭

Ship my order to:

Child's Name _____ Age _____

Parent's Name _____

Street Address* _____

City _____ State/Prov _____ Zip Code _____

*Note: UPS will not deliver to a PO box

Mail this order form (with your check if you're ordering other products) to:

Mainstay Church Resources, Box 30, Wheaton, IL 60189-0030
In Canada: The Chapel Ministries, Box 2000, Waterdown, ON LoR 2Ho

For VISA, MasterCard, or Discover Card orders, call 1-800-224-2735 (U.S.) or 1-800-461-4114 (Canada).

M089CC